ULTIMATE
MACHINES

First published in 2012 by
Miles Kelly Publishing Ltd
Harding's Barn, Bardfield End Green,
Thaxted, Essex, CM6 3PX, UK

Copyright © Miles Kelly Publishing Ltd 2011

© 2012 Discovery Communications, LLC.
Discovery Explore Your World™ and the
Discovery Explore Your World™ logo are
trademarks of Discovery Communications, LLC,
used under license. All rights reserved.
yourdiscovery.com

10 9 8 7 6 5 4 3 2 1

Publishing Director Belinda Gallagher
Creative Director Jo Cowan
Managing Editors Amanda Askew,
  Rosie McGuire
Managing Designer Simon Lee
Proofreaders Carly Blake, Claire Philip
Production Manager Elizabeth Collins
Image Manager Liberty Newton
Reprographics Stephan Davis

ISBN 978-1-84810-511-9

Printed in China

British Library Cataloguing-in-Publication Data
A catalogue record for this book is available
from the British Library

Made with paper from a sustainable forest

www.mileskelly.net
info@mileskelly.net

www.factsforprojects.com

ACKNOWLEDGMENTS

The publishers would like to thank the following sources for the use
of their photographs:

KEY Fotolia=F, Getty Images=GI, istockphoto.com=iS, Rex Features=RF,
Science Photo Library=SPL, Shutterstock=S
t=top, a=above, b=bottom/below, c=center, l=left, r=right, f=far, m=main,
bg=background

COVER Michael Stokes/S BACK COVER Jose Gil/S 1 AHMAD FAIZAL YAHYA/S
2 Pedro Nogueira/S 3(bg) Alexander Vasilyev/S (strip, left to right) Eugene
Berman/S, Christopher Halloran/S, Andrea Danti/S, Brett Mulcahy/S
4–5 1971yes/S 6–7(b) KPA/Zuma/RF 6(m) Corbis, (bl) AridOcean/S, (panel)
Anan Kaewkhammul/S 7(tl) Space Frontiers/Stringer/GI, (tr) studio online/S
8–9(bg) Neo Edmund/S 8(metal) caesart/S, (m) South West News
Service/RF, (r) Eky Studio/S, (bl) Peter Menzel/SPL, (br) akiyoko/S
9(t) National Geographic/GI, (b) Issei Kato/Reuters/Corbis 10–1(t) David
Griffin/Icon SMI/Corbis 10(bl) Robert Young/S, (flag) Stephen Aaron
Rees/S, (b) David Allio/Icon SMI/Corbis 11(tr) kobi nevo/S, (bl) Brian
Bahr/Stringer/GI 12–3(bg) Dariush M./S, (m) Icon Images/RF, (border)
Gordan/S, (b) Tischenko Irina/S 13(br) Kesu/S 14–5(bg) Peter J. Kovacs/S
14(tl) apostol/S, (tr) Henry Groskinsky/Time & Life Pictures/GI, (b) Terence
Dewaele/AFP/GI 15(t) Norbert Wu/GI, (c) Jon Freeman/RF, (b) Georges de
Keerle/Sygma/Corbis 16–7(m) racefotos2008/S 17(tr) Carl de
Souza/AFP/GI, (tracks) hugolacasse/S, (bl) hoboton/S, (br) AFP/GI,
(spikes) Rolf Kosecki/Corbis 18–9(bg) 4designersart/S 18(t) Mai/Mai/Time
Life Pictures/GI, (b) George Steinmetz/Corbis 19(t) Jim Watson/AFP/GI,
(bl) Ethan Miller/GI, (br) Ed Oudenaarden/epa/Corbis 20–1(m) Jonathan
Hordle/RF, (ticket panels) George Pappas/S, (pipe panels) Zlatko Guzmic/S
20(l) GI 21(r) Debbie Egan-Chin/NY Daily News Archive via GI,
(inset) Joe McNally/GI 22–3(m) Michael Stokes/S 22(tl) Presniakov
Oleksandr/S, (bl) Jose Gil/S, (br) 808isgreat/S 23(tr) Sipa Press/RF,

(bl) Mighty Sequoia Studio/S, (negative) Hintau Aliaksei/S,
(br) RTimages/S 24–5(b, bg) archetype/S, (t, bg) R-studio/S, (m) Yuriko
Nakao/Reuters/Corbis, (border) gorica/S 24(b) Michael Caronna/Bloomberg
via GI, (b, frame) Maria Toutoudaki/iS 25(t) Dmitry Nikolajchuk/S, (b) Bill
Pugliano/GI 26–7(border) S, (m) Jessica Rinaldi/Reuters/Corbis, (labels) S
26(bg) Anteromite/S, (t) Leo Francini/S, (c) Jakub Krechowicz/S, (b) Mark
Carrel/S 27(tr) USCG/SPL, (br) pashabo/S 28–9(m) Master Sgt. Kevin J.
Gruenwald/RF 29(bl) Corbis, (bl, bg) Ana de Sousa/S 30(t) The Labor
Shed/S, (panels) James Nemec/S, (bl, frame) frescomovie/S 30–1(bg) Sasha
Buzko/S, (c) MarketOlya/S, (clockwise starting bl) Jakub Krechowicz/S,
Bettmann/Corbis, GI, Time & Life Pictures/GI, SSPL/GI, Zdenko Hirschler/RF,
Curventa/RF 32(t) Kai Forsterling/epa/Corbis 33(cl) Justin Sullivan/GI, (cr) nikkytok/S, (b) U.S.
Coast Guard – digital ve/Science Faction/Corbis 34–5(bg) Hywit Dimyadi/S,
(b) yuyangc/S, (tl) Erik Viktor/SPL, (bl) Linali/S, (c) NASA/SPL,
(tr) NASA/SPL, (br) NASA/SPL 36–7(bg) Molodec/S, (m) Du Huaju/Xinhua
Press/Corbis, (panels) Stefan Delle/S 36(t) Reuters/Corbis, (bl) RF,
(br, paper) pdtnc/F, (br, sign) Raia/S 37(t) Reuters/Corbis, (c) Vitaly
Korovin/S 38–9 (bg, metal) R-studio/S, (bg, ipad) Viktor Gmyria/S,
(panels) S 38(t) Andrea Danti/S, (bl) AFP/GI, (br) Bloomberg via GI
39(l) Detlev Van Ravenswaay/SPL, (l, frame) Dic Liew/S, (r) News
Pictures/MCP/RF

All other photographs are from: Corel, digitalSTOCK, digitalvision,
Dreamstime.com, Fotolia.com, iStockphoto.com, John Foxx, PhotoAlto,
PhotoDisc, PhotoEssentials, PhotoPro, Stockbyte

Every effort has been made to acknowledge the source and copyright
holder of each picture. The publishers apologise for any unintentional
errors or omissions.

ULTIMATE
MACHINES

Clive Gifford
Consultant: John Farndon

Miles Kelly

CONTENTS

◀ The Russian spacecraft, the *Buran*, completed one unmanned flight in 1988. It successfully completed two orbits of Earth in its 206-minute-long mission.

ROCKETING Away

Rockets are the ultimate escape artists. Not only do they leave Earth, overcoming its strong pull of gravity, they also carry their own weight, huge amounts of fuel, and a payload—the satellite, astronauts, or probe that needs to be taken into space. In order to achieve this astounding feat, rockets need to generate awesome amounts of power.

◀ The space shuttle, *Columbia*, blasts off, propelled by its pair of gigantic rocket boosters. The boosters drop away from the shuttle about two minutes after liftoff.

Preparing for liftoff

After being carefully assembled and triple-checked, a rocket is carried on a large, slow-moving crawler transporter to its launchpad. Raised upright, beside a tall launch gantry, the rocket is filled with fuel and its launch sequence is programmed. As the final countdown finishes, the rocket engines start. They use fuel at an alarming rate. An engine on *Saturn V* used 1,738 lb (788 kg) of fuel every second—enough to power 260 *Boeing 747* airliners—as well as 3,945 lb (1,789 kg) of liquid oxygen.

TOP 5 TALLEST ROCKETS

SATURN V (USA)
363 ft (110 m)

N1 (SOVIET UNION)
345 ft (104 m)

ARES I-X (USA)
327 ft (100 m)

DELTA IV HEAVY (USA)
235 ft (72 m)

ANGARA A5/KVRB (RUSSIA)
209 ft (64 m)

NASA'S NEW ATLAS V ROCKET STANDS 191 FT (58 M) HIGH AND WEIGHS 737,400 LB (334,500 KG).

▼ A new solid-fuel *Ares 1* rocket engine is tested on the ground, generating an awesome 3.6 million lb (1.6 million kg) of thrust. The rocket is 154 ft (47 m) tall and consumes about 700,000 lb (320,000 kg) of fuel per minute.

GETTING A BOOST

One way to give spacecraft a push at liftoff is to use boosters—solid-fuel rockets containing a mixture of fuel and oxidizer that fire up at launch time. Each booster is used up quite quickly—*Ariane 5*'s boosters lasted for just 130 seconds. The boosters then eject from the main spacecraft, reducing its weight as it heads into space.

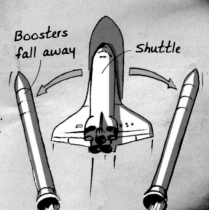

Boosters fall away

Shuttle

Massive engine thrust

Rocket engines can generate huge power. *Saturn V* sent U.S. astronauts to the Moon between 1969 and 1973. Its five F1 rocket engines each produced 1.5 million lb (700,000 kg) of thrust—roughly the same amount of power created by half a million sports cars! The F1 engines ran for just 2.5 minutes, but in that time they blasted *Saturn V* to a height of 42 mi (68 km) above Earth. As their fuel ran out, the engines were jettisoned with the spacecraft zooming at more than 6,160 mph (9,915 km/h).

Saturn V, carrying the Apollo 15 lunar mission, lifts off from Kennedy Space Center. The rocket burned 4.4 million lb (2 million kg) of fuel during the first 150 seconds of operation.

ROBERT GODDARD LAUNCHED THE FIRST LIQUID-FUELED ROCKET IN 1926. IT WAS 11.2 FT (3.4 M) TALL AND WEIGHED JUST 6 LB (2.7 KG).

Mixing it up

A rocket engine needs oxygen to work but there is no oxygen in space. When they are in Earth's atmosphere, rockets cannot draw in air like a jet engine does. Rockets solve this problem by carrying thousands of gallons of oxidizer (oxygen-making substances). When oxidizer is mixed with fuel and burned, huge amounts of hot, high pressure gases leave the rocket nozzles, often at speeds of more than 12,000 ft (3,800 m) per second.

Droids in
DANGER

Some robots work in locations or situations too risky or difficult for humans to explore or perform tasks. These include places where poisonous chemical spills, radioactive leaks, or crumbling earthquake-damaged buildings would harm or even kill people.

▼ A British Army bomb disposal bot moves closer to a car that is suspected to contain a real bomb.

Bomb bots

Sent to investigate unexploded ordnance such as mines or bombs, bomb disposal bots take measurements and close-up photos, and send them back to human experts a safe distance away. Their extendable arms can be fitted with a range of tools, including claws to lift and carry a suspicious package, and water disrupters, which blast water into a bomb to scramble its circuits before it can detonate.

Rescue robots

When disaster strikes, robots help to locate survivors and investigate the most risky parts of an accident site. Some robots can wriggle their way through pipes or rubble. They can detect dangerous gases or spot signs of life among wreckages. Their microcameras send images to rescue workers on the surface. Rescue robots were used to seek out victims after the 2001 World Trade Center disaster and after Hurricane Katrina struck in New Orleans, U.S., in 2005. They also helped after the Crandall Canyon mine disaster in Utah, U.S., in 2007.

▼ A rescue robot clambers over rubble using its jointed sets of tracks, and a CCD camera sensor scans the terrain in front of it.

▶ Robot submersibles can deploy bait cages to attract animals for observation and research.

Deep divers

Unmanned machines can dive for long periods of time—without having to supply large amounts of oxygen for any crew to breathe. They can be built small to get into difficult areas and are used to examine dangerous parts of the ocean floor, such as undersea volcanoes and plane and ship wreckages. The *Jason* ROV (Remotely Operated Vehicle) explored the wreck of *Titanic* more than 2.5 mi (4 km) below the surface of the Atlantic Ocean.

Fire! Fire!

Heat, toxic smoke, and the threat of a burning building crashing down makes fighting fires one of the most dangerous jobs in the world. Robots are being developed to tackle blazes alongside human firefighters. Some robots, such as *Firerob* and *FFR1*, are designed to get close to major infernos. *Firerob* can withstand temperatures that would fry people—up to 2,280°F (1,250°C).

▲ *Guardrobo D1* patrols buildings, detecting changes of temperature and smoke to find small fires. It can then put them out with its own fire extinguisher.

Dramatic
DRAGSTERS

No cars accelerate faster than dragsters. Pairs of these speed machines race each other down a long, narrow ribbon of track called a drag strip. Races are over a distance of either a quarter of a mile (402 m) or an eighth of a mile (201 m). With the fastest dragsters, the race is over in under five seconds. Blink and you really will miss it.

▶ Two Top Fuel dragsters power down the strip at Las Vegas Motor Speedway, U.S. Drivers have to steady their vehicles, which shudder under the extreme power.

Top Fuel machines

The National Hot Rod Association is where the top dragster operators race, and the fastest of all are Top Fuel machines. These long, thin vehicles are made of a tubular steel frame with a wheelbase (the distance between the front and rear wheels) of 180–300 in (457–762 cm)—three times the length of a normal car. The powerful engines are mounted between the large rear wheels and are fueled by racing alcohol, which is an explosive mixture of nitromethane and methanol. This mixture generates more than three times the power of regular gasoline. About 16 gal (60.5 l) of fuel is used in one race.

ALMOST 8,000 HORSEPOWER IS GENERATED BY A TOP FUEL DRAGSTER ENGINE—THAT'S MORE THAN TEN NASCARS ON THE STARTING GRID OF THE DAYTONA 500.

▼ This Top Fuel racer's wheels spin as it prepares to leave the start line. A Top Fuel dragster accelerates from 0 to more than 300 mph (480 km/h) in less time than it takes to read this sentence!

LAYING RUBBER

SHORTLY BEFORE A RACE, DRAGSTERS SPIN THEIR REAR WHEELS HARD, GENERATING MASSES OF SMOKE AND LAYING DOWN TWO PATCHES OF RUBBER ON THE TRACK, ONE FROM EACH WHEEL. THIS IS CALLED A BURNOUT AND REMOVES ANY DEBRIS FROM THE TIRE SURFACE. IT ALSO HEATS UP THE TIRES, WHICH MAKES THEIR SURFACE STICKIER AND BETTER AT GRIPPING THE TRACK AT THE START OF THE RACE.

In 2005, Tony Schumacher reached a record speed of 336.15 mph (540.97 km/h) and completed the race in 4.4 seconds.

Fast finish

In seconds, the race is over, with the dragsters hitting top speed shortly before crossing the finish line. The driver applies powerful brakes and releases one or two drag parachutes. These billow out behind the vehicle, causing air resistance, which slows down the dragster.

◀ With the race over, it's time to slow down—and fast! The driver applies the rear brakes using a lever in the cockpit and deploys the pair of drag chutes.

IT TAKES 0.8 SECONDS FOR A DRAGSTER TO ACCELERATE FROM 0 TO MORE THAN 100 MPH (160 KM/H).

ROBO-ZILLA!

Some machines are not built to save lives or provide transport, they are purely for entertainment. Many such robots come in the form of pets such as Sony's *AIBO*, a robotic dog that responds to voice commands. Other machines are built to be more brutal. They are designed to stun, surprise, and even shock people. These are the extreme entertainment machines.

Robosaurus stands a massive 42 ft (13 m) high

The spiked tail is 30 ft (9 m) high

VICTIM LIST

* CARS
* BOATS
* JETS
* TRUCKS
* LIGHT AIRCRAFT

DREADFUL DINOSAURS

A number of robotic dinosaurs have been built to wow and scare visitors to theme parks, museums, and other attractions. Some are remote controled, meaning that a human operator guides their movements from a short distance away. Others might be preprogrammed to repeat a series of movements.

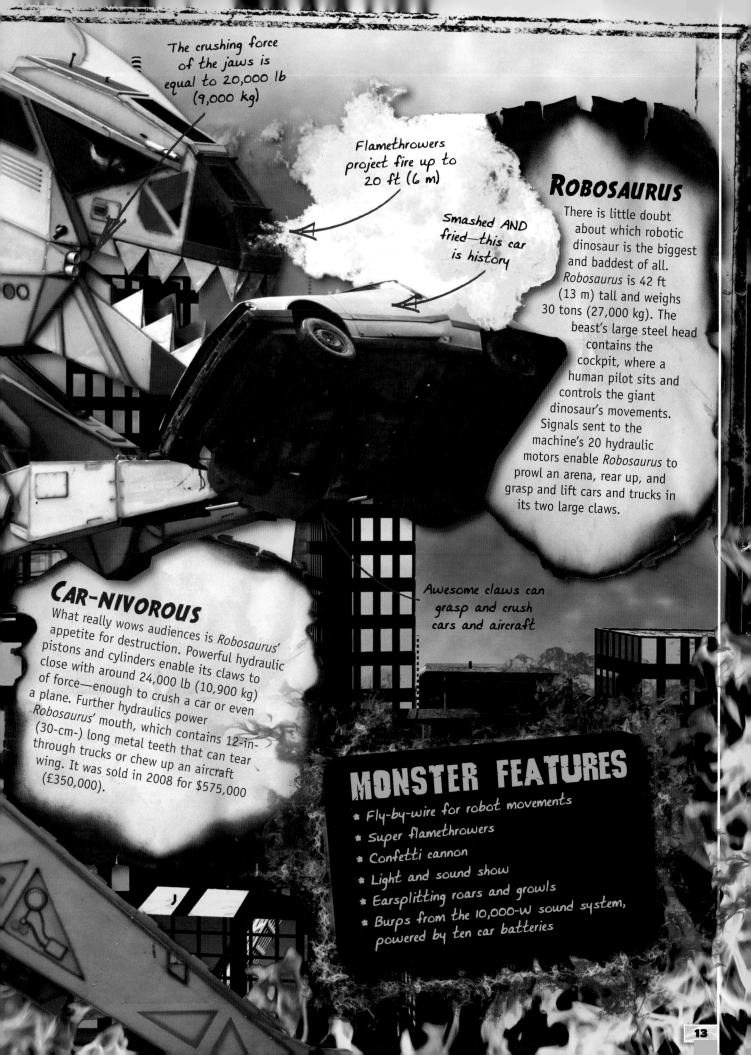

The crushing force of the jaws is equal to 20,000 lb (9,000 kg)

Flamethrowers project fire up to 20 ft (6 m)

Smashed AND fried—this car is history

ROBOSAURUS

There is little doubt about which robotic dinosaur is the biggest and baddest of all. *Robosaurus* is 42 ft (13 m) tall and weighs 30 tons (27,000 kg). The beast's large steel head contains the cockpit, where a human pilot sits and controls the giant dinosaur's movements. Signals sent to the machine's 20 hydraulic motors enable *Robosaurus* to prowl an arena, rear up, and grasp and lift cars and trucks in its two large claws.

CAR-NIVOROUS

What really wows audiences is *Robosaurus'* appetite for destruction. Powerful hydraulic pistons and cylinders enable its claws to close with around 24,000 lb (10,900 kg) of force—enough to crush a car or even a plane. Further hydraulics power *Robosaurus'* mouth, which contains 12-in- (30-cm-) long metal teeth that can tear through trucks or chew up an aircraft wing. It was sold in 2008 for $575,000 (£350,000).

Awesome claws can grasp and crush cars and aircraft

MONSTER FEATURES

* Fly-by-wire for robot movements
* Super flamethrowers
* Confetti cannon
* Light and sound show
* Earsplitting roars and growls
* Burps from the 10,000-w sound system, powered by ten car batteries

Diving
DOWN

Submersibles and submarines are able to dive down, carrying people and scientific equipment to explore the ocean depths. Many submersibles have found treasure, bombs, or parts of planes. The deeper they dive, the higher the water pressure, so the tougher subs need to be. At 7,000 ft (2,100 m) down, an unprotected submarine would be crushed like a tin can.

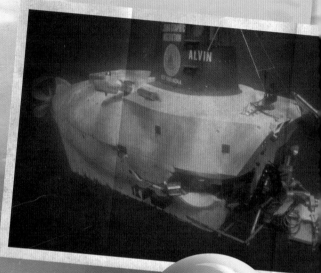

Name: *Alvin*
Deepest dive:
14,764 ft (4,500 m)
Size: 23 ft (7 m) x 8.5 ft
(2.6 m) x 12 ft (4 m)
Used for: Deep-ocean
exploration

Name: *Scubster*
Deepest dive:
19.7 ft (6 m)
Size: 13.8 ft (4.2 m)
x 7.8 ft (2.4 m)
Used for: Shallow water
scuba diving
operations

Pedal power
This amazing French mini-sub has no engine. Instead, it is pedal-powered by its pilot. Hard pedaling turns the two sets of fan blades, which can move the craft forward at a cruising speed of 6 mph (10 km/h). A large, clear canopy gives wonderful underwater views.

Searching the deep

Deep Flight 1 carries just one person who lies face down. It can stay underwater for up to four hours. Its six external lights brighten the murky depths, allowing the craft's four cameras to take amazing images of ocean life.

IN 1960, THE TRIESTE SUB REACHED THE BOTTOM OF THE DEEPEST PART OF THE PACIFIC OCEAN, A DEPTH OF ABOUT 35,800 FT (10,900 M).

Name:
Deep Flight 1
Deepest dive: 3,000 ft (914 m)
Size: 13 ft (4 m) x 8 ft (2.5 m)
Used for: Deep-ocean exploration and photography

Flying through water

Most submarines have large ballast tanks that are either filled with water to dive down or emptied to rise up. However, *Deep Flight Aviator* uses upside-down wings! The wings work like the wings of a plane, but in reverse, driving the sub down through the water at speeds up to 330 ft (100 m) per minute. This two-person submersible also has twin cockpits, allowing a navigator or trainee pilot to practice their skills.

Name:
Deep Flight Aviator
Deepest dive: 1,500 ft (457 m)
Size: 22 ft (7 m) x 12 ft (4 m) x 6 ft (2 m)
Used for: Submersible pilot training and research

Name: *Typhoon*
Deepest dive: 1,312 ft (400 m)
Size: 560 ft (170 m) long
Used for: Carrying nuclear ballistic missiles

Mega subs

Built in the 1970s, the Soviet Union's *Typhoon* Class Submarine wasn't the deepest diver, but at more than 560 ft (170 m) long, it was definitely the largest. Completely empty of fuel, crew, and supplies, it weighed a staggering 44 million lb (20 million kg). Housing 150 crew, the submarine was powered by two nuclear power reactors and carried 20 missiles, as well as torpedoes, which could be used against enemy ships. The submarine could stay underwater for 120 days at a time.

BLISTERING Bikes

Motorbikes are one of the most versatile types of motor vehicle. They can be built to cruise long distances on roads in comfort, race around tracks, or climb and jump over rough offroad terrain. The fastest bikes, such as MotoGP machines, can race at speeds close to 200 mph (322 km/h).

IN 2009, MOTOGP'S DANI PEDROSA REACHED A RECORD SPEED OF 217.037 MPH (349.288 KM/H) ON A HONDA BIKE.

▼ Two MotoGP bikes roar around a fast turn on a race circuit. The riders' knee hovers just fractions of an inch above the track surface.

Lean angle

Motorbike riders learn to shift their body weight on their motorbike saddle to control their machine and stay balanced. Riders lean into corners so that the bike turns with them. In motorcycle racing, riders take corners at high speed so have to lean close to the track, with their knees protected by plastic or metal guards called knee sliders.

Muddy machines

Motocross machines are tough enough to survive an offroad bashing. Racing over muddy or dirt circuits with hills, ditches, bumps, and tight turns, a motocross bike has a rugged frame and a powerful suspension system to keep the wheels on the ground as much as possible, while a cord called a kill switch attaches the rider to the bike's engine ignition. Should the rider fall off, the bike's engine is cut and stops.

▶ A staggering 1,250 motocross riders take part in the Weston beach race in the U.K. The bike tires have a rough, knobbly outer surface to help them grip in the loose sand.

THE SUZUKI HAYABUSA CAN GO FROM 0 TO 60 MPH (96 KM/H) IN JUST 2.7 SECONDS. THE BIKE HAS A TOP SPEED OF AROUND 186 MPH (299 KM/H).

Ice Speedway

Motorcycle speedway sees four bikes race around a tight oval dirt track. The action is intense and the bikes have no brakes, but that isn't extreme enough for some speedway riders. They choose to race on ovals covered with a layer of frozen ice. Ice bikes can reach a speed of 80 mph (130 km/h).

An Ice Speedway rear tire has 200–300 spikes that are one inch (2.5 cm) long to grip the ice.

Secret SPYBOTS

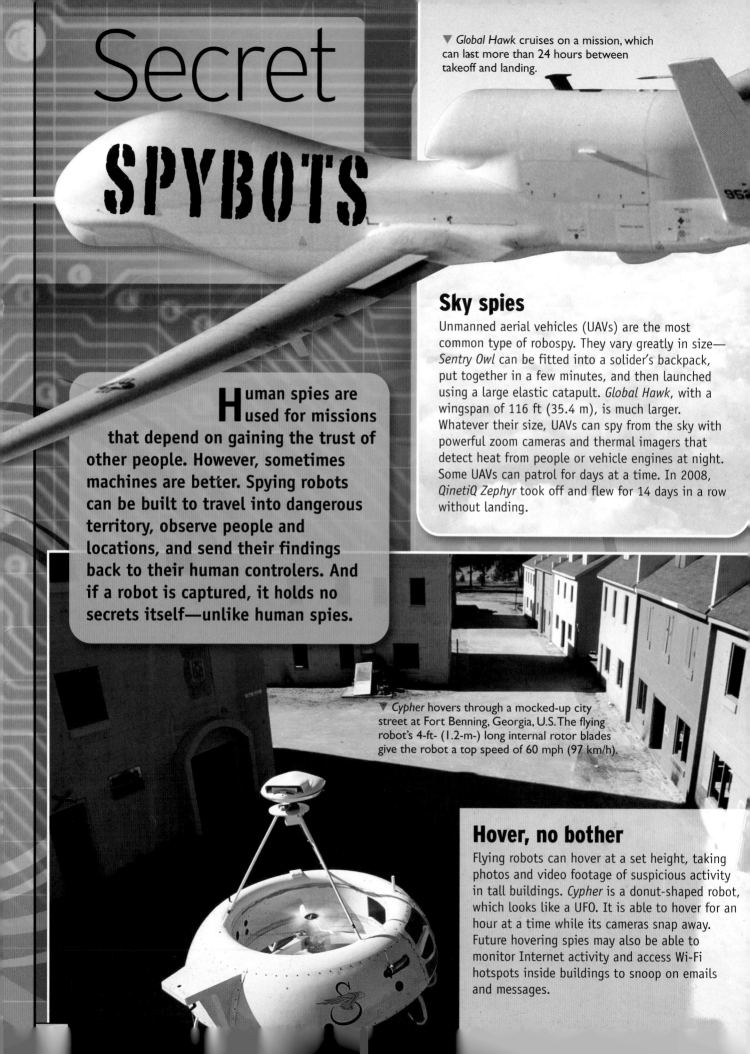

▼ *Global Hawk* cruises on a mission, which can last more than 24 hours between takeoff and landing.

Human spies are used for missions that depend on gaining the trust of other people. However, sometimes machines are better. Spying robots can be built to travel into dangerous territory, observe people and locations, and send their findings back to their human controlers. And if a robot is captured, it holds no secrets itself—unlike human spies.

Sky spies

Unmanned aerial vehicles (UAVs) are the most common type of robospy. They vary greatly in size— *Sentry Owl* can be fitted into a solider's backpack, put together in a few minutes, and then launched using a large elastic catapult. *Global Hawk*, with a wingspan of 116 ft (35.4 m), is much larger. Whatever their size, UAVs can spy from the sky with powerful zoom cameras and thermal imagers that detect heat from people or vehicle engines at night. Some UAVs can patrol for days at a time. In 2008, *QinetiQ Zephyr* took off and flew for 14 days in a row without landing.

▼ *Cypher* hovers through a mocked-up city street at Fort Benning, Georgia, U.S. The flying robot's 4-ft- (1.2-m-) long internal rotor blades give the robot a top speed of 60 mph (97 km/h).

Hover, no bother

Flying robots can hover at a set height, taking photos and video footage of suspicious activity in tall buildings. *Cypher* is a donut-shaped robot, which looks like a UFO. It is able to hover for an hour at a time while its cameras snap away. Future hovering spies may also be able to monitor Internet activity and access Wi-Fi hotspots inside buildings to snoop on emails and messages.

Looking ahead

Some covert operations take place on the ground. Tracked crawler robots can be ordered to travel ahead of police or troops. Using cameras and sensors that can detect explosive chemicals, these robots can send back pictures and information using wireless communications to people a safe distance away. Robots such as *Packbot* and *Matilda*, which have telescopic arms, have been used to spy on people in caves, tunnels, and buildings in Iraq. They've alerted troops to lethal surprises ahead, from booby trap bombs to landmines and enemy soldiers in hiding.

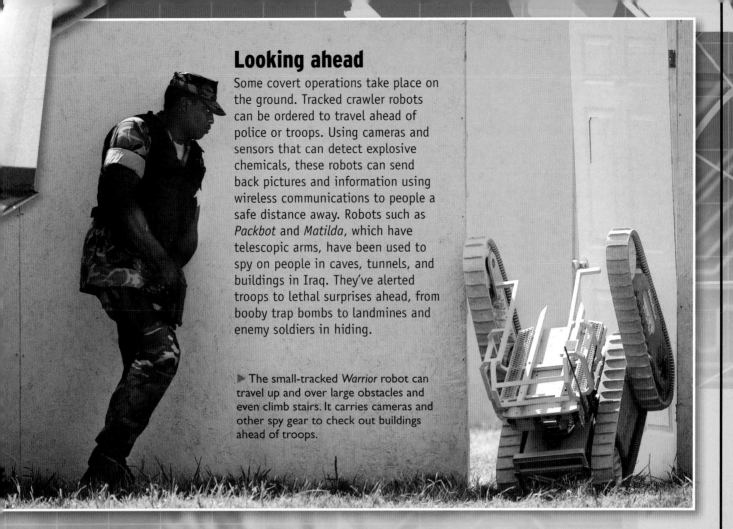

▶ The small-tracked *Warrior* robot can travel up and over large obstacles and even climb stairs. It carries cameras and other spy gear to check out buildings ahead of troops.

▼ Using cameras and microphones, a *WowWee Rovio* transmits what it sees and hears to its owner, who can be hundreds of miles away.

Home alone?

Having your own home spy is no longer science fiction. Robots including *Fujitsu Maron-1*, *Tmsuk Banyru*, and *WowWee Rovio* can act as spies at home. Their sensors can detect unexpected movement, while cameras can film intruders, record what they say, and then transmit this information over the Internet to the homeowner.

Insect agents

Micro Aerial Vehicles (MAVs) are flying robots made to the scale of living insects. They are capable of carrying both tiny cameras and listening devices that are able to record conversations and relay them back to their base via radio signals. Built cheaply and in large numbers, future squadrons of MAVs might be able to swarm over large areas, searching for particular chemical substances or a person whose face matches the one held in their memories.

◀ The *Delfly* robot carries a tiny camera and weighs just 0.1 oz (3 g). It flaps its wings to keep airborne.

White-knuckle RIDES

When it comes to providing extreme thrills at a theme park, a mega roller coaster cannot be beaten. Consisting of a train of carriages whizzing around a large track, a roller coaster uses sudden changes of speed, dizzying heights, and gut-churning twists to provide you with the ultimate, adrenaline-packed white-knuckle ride.

▶ Hundreds of thrillseekers can ride the twisting, looping *Colossus* roller coaster at Thorpe Park, U.K., every hour.

▶ The 2,260-ft- (690-m-) long *Infusion* in Blackpool, U.K., suspends passengers in chairs hanging from the track.

Hanging around

On some rides such as *Anaconda* in Virginia, U.S., the cars hang from below the track. This can give an exhilarating and scary view of the ground below. On the *Superman Ultimate Flight* roller coasters in New Jersey and Georgia, U.S., the cars tilt so that passengers hang facedown, their bodies parallel to the ground, as they race along at 60 mph (96 km/h)—just like flying superheroes.

Power trips

Roller coasters use a variety of different power systems to launch the ride and build up speed. Modern roller coasters, such as *Kingda Ka* in New Jersey, U.S., use a hydraulic launch mechanism, in which mighty hydraulic pumps power a winch that pulls the roller coaster train at fearsome speed. People on the ride find themselves hurtling down the track at an extreme speed of 128 mph (206 km/h). And all that takes place in just 3.5 seconds!

▼ Mean and green, the *Kingda Ka* ride takes just 59 seconds from start to finish.

Twist and turn

A roller coaster track loops and turns through various types of bend. Some are sharply banked (angled in or out) to make it feel like you are falling over the edge of the track. Others are tight hairpin turns, which the train whizzes through at high speed. The ultimate turn, called an inversion, takes you upside down. The simplest of these is a loop-the-loop, where the track travels in a vertical circle. *Colossus* at Thorpe Park, U.K., is not particularly long at 2,789 ft (850 m), but it contains a world-record ten inversions in the one minute and 45 seconds it takes to get from start to finish.

KINGDA KA'S 418-FT (128-M) DROP IS THE BIGGEST IN THE WORLD.

VIEW FROM THE TOP

Big drops

A roller coaster is carefully designed to give the maximum number of safe thrills as possible along its length. Many roller coasters have giant vertical or almost vertical drops from the top of the hill (the highest points on the ride) down to almost ground level. *Top Thrill Dragster* in Ohio, U.S., has a 400-ft (122-m) drop.

DODONPA IN JAPAN IS THE WORLD'S FASTEST ACCELERATING ROLLER COASTER. IT TAKES JUST 1.8 SECONDS TO REACH 106.8 MPH (171.9 KM/H).

Monster TRUCKS

Trucks perform many tasks, such as shifting building materials around construction sites and hauling freight on roads between cities. Some trucks, however, are just built to entertain. Monster trucks appear in arenas and stadiums to perform stunts and jumps, car crushing, and to race over obstacle courses against each other.

▼ Two monster trucks trample old cars in an exciting showdown. Most monster trucks have a top speed of 50–85 mph (80–137 km/h), but some go faster.

HOW BIG IS BIGFOOT 5?

HEIGHT 15.5 ft (4.7 m)

WIDTH 13 ft (3.9 m)

WEIGHT 28,000 lb (12,701 kg)

TIRE WEIGHT 2,400 lb (1,087 kg)

Super stunts

Monster trucks perform some amazing stunts, often in quite small arenas. In 1999, *Bigfoot 14* roared off a ramp and jumped over a *Boeing 727* airliner, recording a massive 202-ft- (61.6-m-) long jump. Drivers wear helmets and flame-retardant racing suits and are strapped securely into their seat with harnesses. Windshields are often made of a clear plastic called Lexan, which does not shatter.

Mighty movers

Monster trucks are built from a tubular steel frame covered in body panels. The body perches high above its giant wheels, riding on a strong suspension system to allow the truck to climb over other vehicles. All four wheels are driven by the engine, and the tires are 5.5 ft (1.7 m) in height and 3.6 ft (1.1 m) wide. The entire vehicle weighs 10,000 lb (4,536 kg).

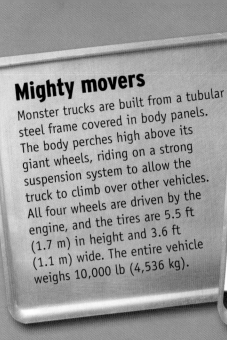

▼ *Bigfoot 5*'s tires are so big, at 10 ft (3 m) in diameter and 4 ft (1.2 m) wide, that children can stand inside the wheels.

▼ *Liebherr T 282B* can carry an enormous load of up to 720,000 lb (327,000 kg).

Big rigs

Even bigger than *Bigfoot* are the giant tipper trucks used in the mining industry to move rock and rubble from place to place. The *Liebherr T 282B* dump truck measures 48 ft (14.5 m) long and 29 ft (8.7 m) wide. Its engine alone weighs more than 20,000 lb (9,091 kg).

A bunch of dummies

Crash test dummies are models of real people placed inside cars or on motorbikes so that testers can record and analyze the effects of a crash on people. Dummies come in all different sizes, representing different ages and genders. Inside each dummy is a rigid structure that mimics parts of the human skeleton. The latest crash test dummies can cost up to $200,000 (£150,000).

CRASH! BANG!

CRASH! Metal crumples, glass shatters, and fabrics shred. There are thousands of car crashes around the world every day. But motor vehicles are getting safer and that's partly down to the work of crash testing centers. They test vehicle models before they go on sale to research how to make them safer.

Crash test benefits

In the past, crash testing has revealed cars that do not protect drivers and passengers, stopping unsafe vehicles going on sale. It has also helped lead to major safety innovations such as side impact bars in car doors and air bags, which inflate rapidly on impact to protect the head of both the driver and the frontseat passenger.

▲ Colored paints on a crash test dummy's face leave marks, showing its impact on an air bag after a crash test.

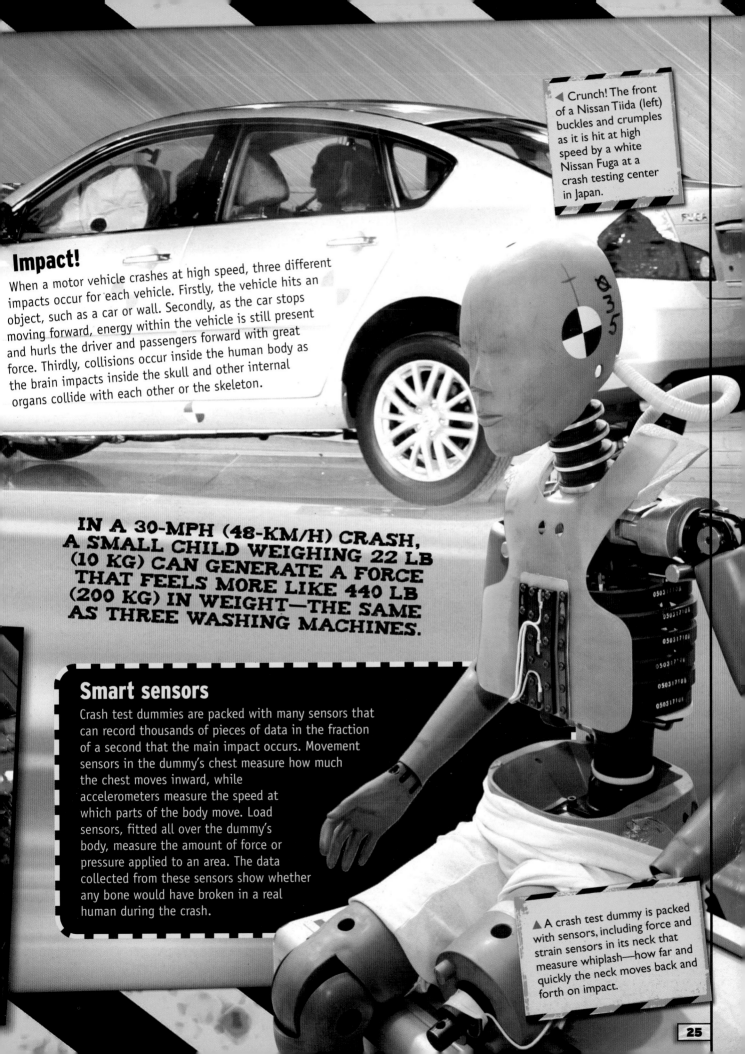

◀ Crunch! The front of a Nissan Tiida (left) buckles and crumples as it is hit at high speed by a white Nissan Fuga at a crash testing center in Japan.

Impact!

When a motor vehicle crashes at high speed, three different impacts occur for each vehicle. Firstly, the vehicle hits an object, such as a car or wall. Secondly, as the car stops moving forward, energy within the vehicle is still present and hurls the driver and passengers forward with great force. Thirdly, collisions occur inside the human body as the brain impacts inside the skull and other internal organs collide with each other or the skeleton.

IN A 30-MPH (48-KM/H) CRASH, A SMALL CHILD WEIGHING 22 LB (10 KG) CAN GENERATE A FORCE THAT FEELS MORE LIKE 440 LB (200 KG) IN WEIGHT—THE SAME AS THREE WASHING MACHINES.

Smart sensors

Crash test dummies are packed with many sensors that can record thousands of pieces of data in the fraction of a second that the main impact occurs. Movement sensors in the dummy's chest measure how much the chest moves inward, while accelerometers measure the speed at which parts of the body move. Load sensors, fitted all over the dummy's body, measure the amount of force or pressure applied to an area. The data collected from these sensors show whether any bone would have broken in a real human during the crash.

▲ A crash test dummy is packed with sensors, including force and strain sensors in its neck that measure whiplash—how far and quickly the neck moves back and forth on impact.

OIL RIGS

Deep-sea

Oil is a crucial substance used as a fuel both in power plants and as gasoline in motor vehicles. It is also a vital raw material in many industries, including the plastics industry. Oil is measured in barrels, with one barrel equal to 42 gal (158.9 l). Every year, the global population uses 30,000 million barrels of oil. The demand is enormous and grows every day, which has led to drilling for oil in water both close to coastlines and much further out to sea. These offshore platforms produce about one fifth of the world's oil.

▶ The Petronius platform in the Gulf of Mexico stands 246 ft (75 m) above the sea surface, but there's a further 1,754 ft (535 m) below the water to the seabed.

Fiery flares

As oil is recovered from beneath the seabed, it is pumped into the rig's many storage tanks. Some rigs have a direct pipeline connection to the shore. Pockets of natural gas are often found when drilling for oil. Some of this gas is used on the rig, and burned to provide heating and hot water for the crew members living there. The remaining gas can either be piped away to be used as fuel or burned off at the flare boom—a long metal arm that sticks out to one side of the platform.

▼ Natural gas found when drilling for oil is burned off from flare booms, such as this one in the Persian Gulf.

The flare boom, jutting out over the ocean, allows pockets of natural gas encountered while

Made of steel, the drilling derrick rises high above the rest of the platform.

The helipad allows people and urgent supplies to be ferried to and from the rig.

Towering high

The tallest part of an oil rig is usually its derrick. This is a strong metal frame that forms a tall tower. The derrick supports the weight of the drill string and the drill bit, which consists of a number of wheels with strong, sharp teeth that rip through the rock to reach the oil. A mixture of water, clay, and chemicals, called mud, is piped down to cool the drill bit as it drills.

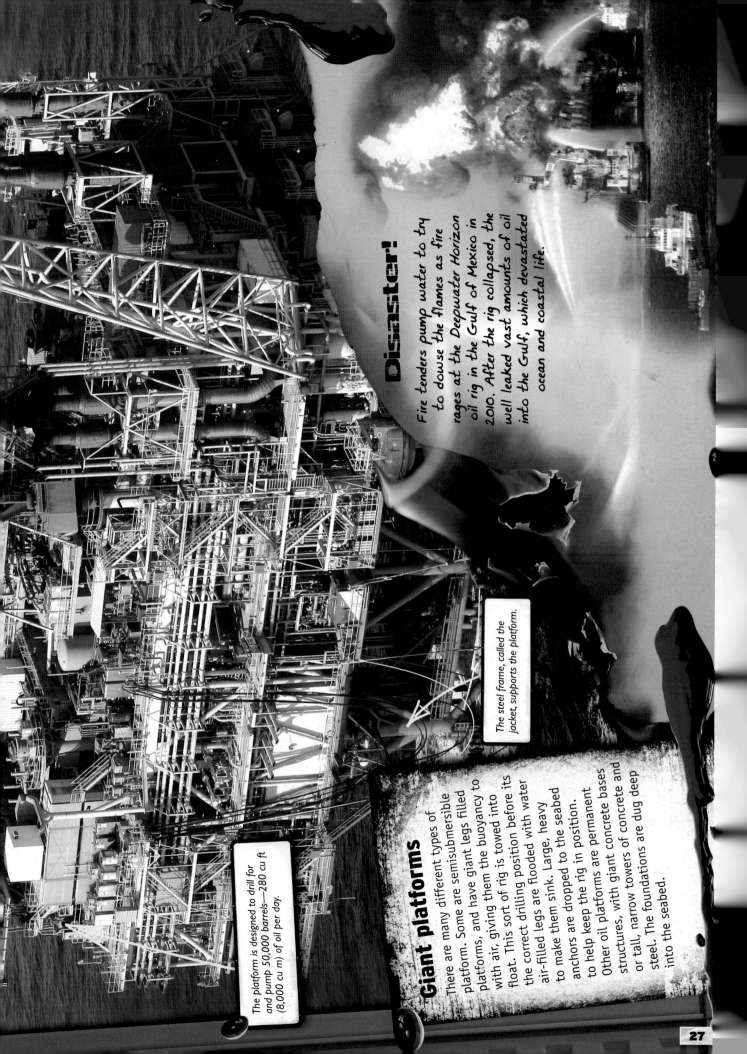

Disaster!

Fire tenders pump water to try to douse the flames as fire rages at the Deepwater Horizon oil rig in the Gulf of Mexico in 2010. After the rig collapsed, the well leaked vast amounts of oil into the Gulf, which devastated ocean and coastal life.

The steel frame, called the jacket, supports the platform.

Giant platforms

There are many different types of platforms. Some are semisubmersible platforms, and have giant legs filled with air, giving them the buoyancy to float. This sort of rig is towed into the correct drilling position before its air-filled legs are flooded with water to make them sink. Large, heavy anchors are dropped to the seabed to help keep the rig in position. Other oil platforms are permanent structures, with giant concrete bases or tall, narrow towers of concrete and steel. The foundations are dug deep into the seabed.

The platform is designed to drill for and pump 50,000 barrels—280 cu ft (8,000 cu m) of oil per day.

JET
POWER

Jets transport millions of passengers on airliners and fly high in the skies as military aircraft. They are powered by extreme engines, which suck in cold air, ignite it with fuel, and eject the hot gases out of the rear to create enormous amounts of thrust.

Fastest flyers

Aircraft with jet engines are some of the fastest planes around. The very fastest jet airliners were *Concorde* and the *TU-144*—the latter had a top speed of 1,550 mph (2,500 km/h). The *F-15 Eagle* military jet's twin engines enabled it to reach a top speed of more than 1,650 mph (2,660 km/h), and the fastest jet plane of all, the *SR71 Blackbird*, could reach 2,200 mph (3,530 km/h).

▲ A *Sea Harrier* uses vectored thrust from four powerful jet nozzles to hover high above the deck of a ship. Flying forward, the jet has a top speed of 735 mph (1,182 km/h).

Straight up

Some aircraft can redirect the flow of hot gases from their jet engines to make them more maneuverable in flight. This is called Vector In Forward Flight or VIFF and is found on the *F35B Lightning* and the *F22 Raptor*. Combat jets can use VIFF to change direction suddenly, crucial in air-to-air combat. Other aircraft use vectored thrust to achieve VTOL (vertical takeoff and landing), sending a 20,755-lb (9,415-kg) *AV8B Harrier* straight up into the air where it can even hover like a helicopter.

AT ITS TOP SPEED, THE F22 RAPTOR COULD FLY FROM NEW YORK CITY TO MIAMI IN LESS THAN 40 MINUTES!

▼ An *F22 Raptor* (top) turns away from an *F15 Eagle* jet. Both aircraft are powered by twin jet engines and have a top speed of more than 1,500 mph (2,410 km/h).

A quick exit

The pilot of a jet can exit his troubled aircraft using an ejection seat. Firstly, the cockpit canopy blasts away before sets of rockets thrust the seat up and out, at least 300 ft (90 m) from the aircraft. At the same time, winglike stabilizer fins fold out to help keep the pilot and seat stable. As the seat blasts away, a small explosive charge detonates in the seat's headrest, forcing open a parachute called a drogue. This slows the seat down and pulls out a much larger main parachute. Once this opens, the seat falls away and the pilot descends safely. Ejection seats have so far saved more than 10,000 lives.

◄ A military jet pilot rockets free of his plane strapped safely into his ejection seat.

POWER UP

Cold air sucked into a jet engine is squeezed to increase its pressure before entering the combustion chamber. Here, it is mixed with fuel and burned, reaching a temperature of about 1,650°F (900°C). This creates rapidly expanding gases, which exit the jet engine through the exhaust nozzle at the rear. The speeding gases create an opposite force, thrusting the aircraft forward.

Cold air sucked into turbojet engine

Expanding hot gases thrust out of the exhaust nozzle

Spinning compressor blades increase air pressure

Air and fuel mixed and ignited in combustion chamber

SPEED Stars

With each advancement in engineering and technology, the speed aces of the day race to design, build, and test-drive new machines that they hope will smash records—and maybe bring them fame and a place in history.

1947: Railton Mobil Special
Bonneville Salt Flats, Utah, U.S.

Powered by two supercharged aircraft engines, Railton was the first land vehicle to break the speed of 400 mph (640 km/h).

1938: Thunderbolt
Bonneville Salt Flats, Utah, U.S.

George Eyston's huge car, Thunderbolt, weighed 7 tons (6,350 kg)—twice that of any of its competitors. It still managed to reach a speed of 357.5 mph (575.3 km/h).

1928: White Triplex
Daytona Beach, Florida, U.S.

Powered by three aircraft engines and driven by Ray Keech, White Triplex reached a top speed of 207.5 mph (334 km/h) on Florida's Daytona Beach.

400
300
200
100
0 mph

400
200
0 km/h

Malcolm Campbell's son Donald followed in his father's risky footsteps, setting a new record of 403.8 mph (648.7 km/h).

1964: Bluebird CN7
Lake Eyre, Australia

1970: Blue Flame
Bonneville Salt Flats, Utah, U.S.

THE BLUE FLAME

Blue Flame sets a new record, averaging a scorching 630.4 mph (1,014.5 km/h) on Bonneville Salt Flats.

1997: Thrust SSC
Black Rock Desert, Nevada, U.S.

The first land vehicle to go faster than the speed of sound was driven by fighter pilot Andy Green. It clocked an average speed of 763 mph (1,228 km/h).

2012: Bloodhound SSC,
Hakskeenpan, South Africa

This new car will be powered by a rocket bolted to a Eurofighter-Typhoon jet engine. The team behind it hopes to reach a speed of 1,000 mph (1,610 km/h).

To the RESCUE

▼ A *Bombardier 415* dumps 1,620 gal (6,140 l) of water from its hold onto a raging forest fire.

When an emergency call is taken or an emergency signal given out, technology is at work from the start. Communications centers and call centers use satellite links, radio, and even Internet connections to alert staff and other services such as the police or mountain rescue. This allows the services to plan and coordinate their actions quickly.

Water bombs

Some fires across dry scrubland or forests can rage out of control, putting towns and villages at risk and destroying valuable habitats and farmland. Water bombing is the use of aircraft and helicopters to drop large quantities of water on forest fires from above. Some fly between the fire and an airfield to be refilled with water. Other planes such as the *Bombardier 415* scoop up water into their large bodies by flying low over water.

◄ A water bomber flies so low that it skims the surface of the sea, filling its hold with water in less than 15 seconds. It can then fly back to the fire.

Breaking the ice

Icebreakers use powerful engines and their weight to plow through ice to help keep shipping lanes open, or to reach a boat or ship stuck in the ice. An icebreaker's hull is specially built and strengthened to withstand the enormous pressures of crunching through ice.

▼ The *L'Astrolabe* ship breaks through some ice on its way to the Antarctic coast. The ship carries a crew of 12 and up to 50 passengers.

▼ Using a thermal imager, a person lying on the floor can be seen through smoke. The warmest parts of the body, the head and hands, glow brightly.

SEEING THROUGH SMOKE

One of the biggest hazards and obstructions for firefighters is thick, heavy smoke. It's hard to see through and dangerous to be in for any length of time. Firefighters often use small, handheld thermal imagers, which detect infrared waves and build up a heat picture of an area. A human emits different infrared waves to an inanimate object, so the body's outline will stand out clearly from the background on the screen.

◄ A U.S. coastguard winchman descends from a hovering Sikorsky HH-60 helicopter to pick up a survivor at sea. The helicopter can operate on patrols or rescue missions for up to 6.5 hours at a time.

Rapid response

Getting to the site of an emergency as quickly as possible is often a crucial factor in saving lives. Many emergency and rescue services are equipped with small, fast, maneuverable vehicles. Motorized snowmobiles can move quickly across icy land, speedy powerboats zoom across water, and rugged 4x4 offroad vehicles tackle uneven land. Helicopters can access places that are difficult for other forms of transport to reach.

One-way Missions

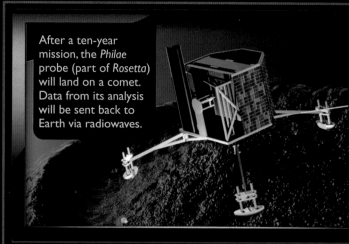

After a ten-year mission, the *Philae* probe (part of *Rosetta*) will land on a comet. Data from its analysis will be sent back to Earth via radiowaves.

Space is a harsh, unforgiving place. There's no air or water, and temperatures can range from an average of -455°F (-255°C) to thousands of degrees when close to the fiery furnace of the Sun. Human beings are just not equipped to survive in space without vast amounts of support equipment and a method of getting back to Earth safely. Space probes, in contrast, are smaller, more compact machines that can withstand the extremes of space and can be sent deep into the Solar System on one-way missions, never to return.

FLY-BYS

Many space probes are designed to fly close by a planet, moon, or comet, so their scientific instruments can take various measurements. Some probes perform more than one fly-by within a single mission. The European Space Agency's *Rosetta* flew by Mars in 2007 and asteroids in 2008 and 2010 on its way to its main mission—to investigate a comet called Churyumov–Gerasimenko, which it will reach in 2014.

LAUNCHED IN 1977, VOYAGER 1 HAS 65,000 WORKING PARTS AND HAS TRAVELED MORE THAN 10.6 BILLION MI (17 BILLION KM) SO FAR.

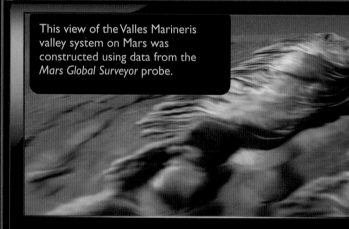

This view of the Valles Marineris valley system on Mars was constructed using data from the *Mars Global Surveyor* probe.

Space probes are expensive, so scientists try to pack as many tasks into the mission as possible. The *Cassini-Huygens* probe made a journey of 2.2 billion mi (3.5 billion km) to Saturn, which took seven years. *Cassini* then orbited Saturn while the smaller probe, Huygens, traveled through the atmosphere of Saturn's largest moon, Titan, taking 700 images before landing. *Huygens'* mission was over in hours but *Cassini's* continues to this day.

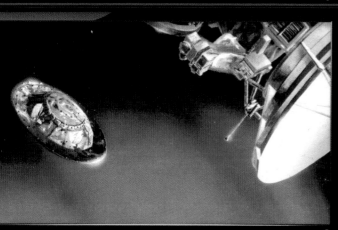

The *Huygens* space probe (left) separates from the *Cassini* space probe shortly before landing on the surface of Saturn's moon, Titan, in 2005.

ORBITERS AND LANDERS

Probes are often classed according to whether they go into orbit around a planet or land on its surface. Both types of probe have been sent to Earth's nearest planetary neighbor, Mars. The first U.S. lander probe on Mars was *Viking I*, which reached the planet in 1976. NASA's *Mars Global Surveyor* began orbiting Mars 21 years later and took a staggering 240,000 digital images of the planet's surface.

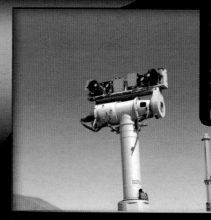

The Mars Exploration Rover, *Opportunity*, landed in 2004 and is still exploring in 2011 having traveled more than 20 mi (32 km) across the planet's surface.

Water FORCE

Electricity is generated in many different ways, from nuclear to coal power plants. Hydroelectric power (HEP) plants harness the power in falling water to turn turbines that generate electricity. The largest and most extreme HEP plant is the Three Gorges Dam in China.

Huge demand

With a population of more than 1.3 billion, China has more people than any other nation and demand for electricity for homes, factories, schools, and offices is soaring. To help fulfil demand, a gigantic dam was built on the powerful Yangtze River, the third longest river in the world at more than 3,900 mi (6,300 km) long.

▶ The dam spans the Yangtze River and is becoming a major tourist attraction in China. Ships can travel past the dam through a series of large locks.

▼ A crowd watches the demolition of buildings in the old city of Fengjie to clear space for the Three Gorges Dam project.

Clearing the way

Work on the Three Gorges Dam began in 1993 and proved to be a massive task. More than 40,000 people worked on its construction day and night. The dam and the reservoir of water it held back covered a vast area of land. More than 80,000 sticks of dynamite were used to blast away rock and clear land and 134 million cu yd (102 million cu m) of earth had to be moved. About 1.4 million people were moved to new homes as hundreds of villages were submerged by the reservoir, which is around 410 mi (660 km) long—the distance from London to Paris and back!

▼ Part of one of the dam's giant electricity generators is lowered into place. Each generator weighs about 13 million lb (6 million kg).

Big results

The dam is simply enormous. It stands 607 ft (185 m) tall and 1.43 mi (2.3 km) wide. It is five times larger than the giant Hoover Dam in the U.S. The dam contains 26 massive electricity generating turbines. In total, they are able to generate around 85 billion kWh of electricity a year. That is almost one tenth of China's electricity needs and equal to electricity produced by up to 15 nuclear power plants. Many of China's other power plants burn coal and the energy produced by the Three Gorges Dam saves 50 million tons (50 billion kg) of coal every year.

THE HIGHEST FLOW OF WATER THROUGH THE DAM IS 10.5 MILLION GAL (40 MILLION L) PER SECOND.

Amazing benefits

The main purpose of the dam is to allow water to flow through turbines to generate electricity. In addition, the dam helps to prevent the Yangtze from flooding its banks and sweeping away homes and entire villages, which has occurred more than 200 times in the last 2,000 years.

◄ Water surges through the dam wall, which is 131 ft (40 m) thick at the top and 377 ft (115 m) thick at the bottom.

Into the FUTURE

No one can be certain what machines and technology we will be using in the future. Less than 15 years ago, for example, there were no iPods, iPhones, or Nintendo Wii, while 30 years ago, there was no broadband, World Wide Web, or CDs. What is certain is that thousands of people are working on exciting new machines around the world, some of which will help the future to become even more extreme.

Really, really small

A nanometer is just over one billionth of a yard or meter. It is so small that a human hair is about 80,000 nanometers in diameter. Nanotechnology is the science of making machines to this incredibly small scale. Advances in nanotechnology may see microscopic machines everywhere—they could repair machines from inside, be woven into smart materials to produce a rollable, pocket computer, or create smart clothes that extend or reduce the fabric depending on the temperature.

▼ In the future, tiny nanorobots may be injected into the body and travel through blood vessels fighting disease directly.

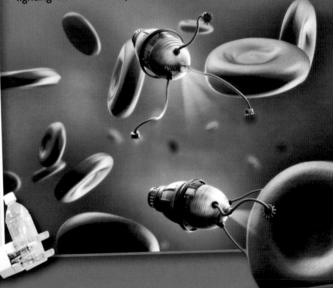

Smarter machines

Computers will continue to get faster, smarter, and smaller. Computing power will be packed into all sorts of machines, from household appliances to cars, which may be capable of self-parking or even self-driving. Robots will become more common and useful in everyday life. Some, with the ability to recognize individual faces and communicate, may become robotic babysitters, store security guards, and even robocops.

▲ Using the cameras in its hands, the *Toshiba ApriAttenda* household robot can open doors and handle items.

▶ General Motors *EN-V* car is a two-seater, two-wheeled electric vehicle that weighs just 900 lb (408 kg). Its sensors can detect obstacles in its path, such as pedestrians or other vehicles, and automatically stop.

Out of this world

In the future, unmanned space probes and robots will venture far into space with increasing frequency. More and more people may get the chance to experience space, staying in space hotels that orbit high above Earth. Humans may use technology to travel further, establishing bases on the Moon or even visiting Mars.

Body machines

More technology will be developed to help repair or improve the performance of the human body. Some of these parts will be controlled directly by a person's brain and nervous system. Sensors in the Cyberdyne Hybrid Assistive Limb (HAL) measure the angle of the knee, hip, and ankle joints, and detect whether the foot is on the floor. It helps people with damaged or weakened legs to walk properly again.

▶ The *Cyberdyne HAL* robot leg can give the wearer up to ten times the strength of a healthy human leg.

▲ Future space hotels may be luxurious orbiting space stations with passenger shuttles ferrying visitors to and from Earth.

INDEX